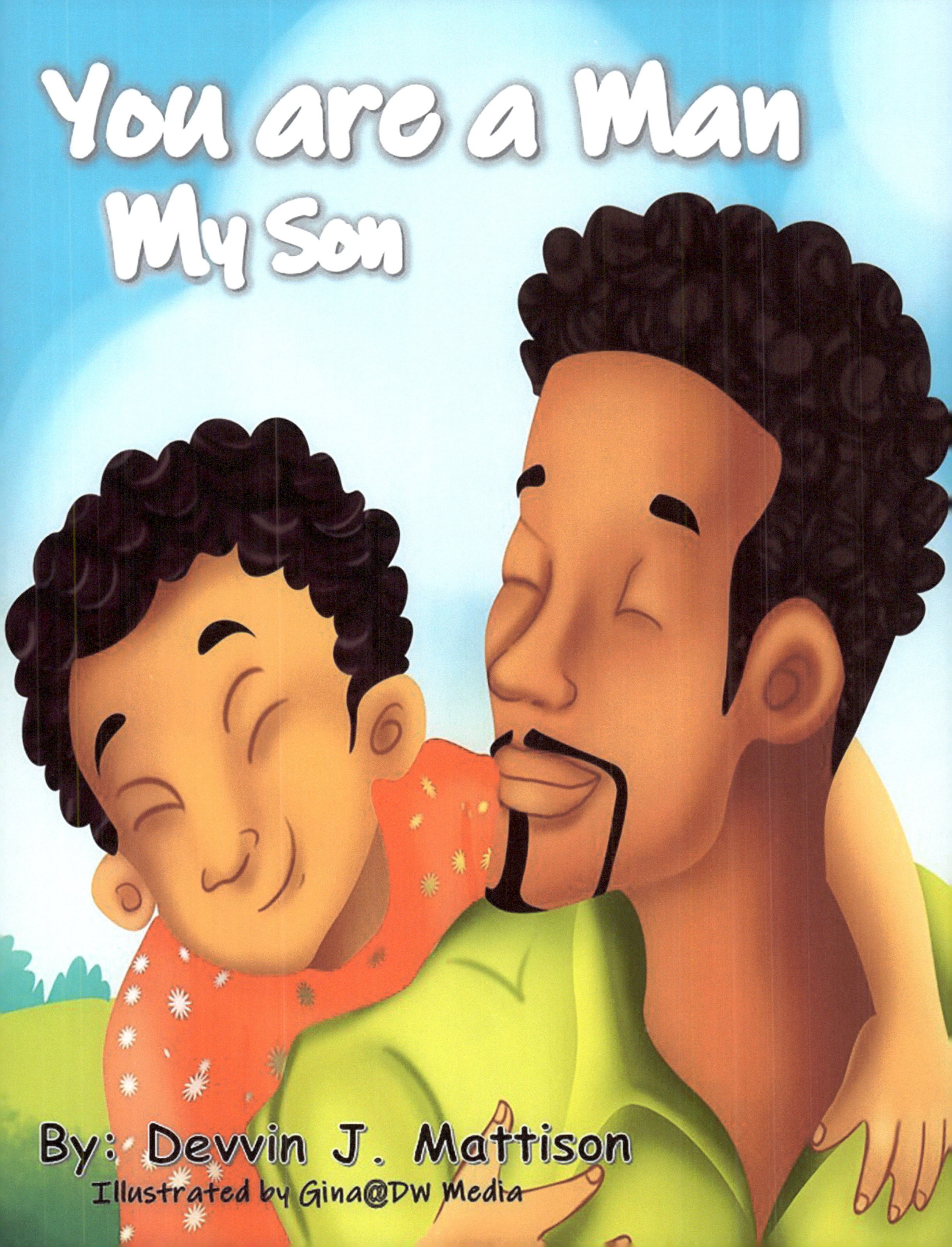

You are a Man My Son

By: Devvin J. Mattison

Illustrated by Gina@DW Media

WORKBOOK PRESS LLC
187 E Warm Springs Rd,
Suite B285, Las Vegas, NV 89119, USA

Website: https://workbookpress.com/
Hotline: 1-888-818-4856
Email: admin@workbookpress.com

Ordering Information:
Quantity sales. Special discounts are available on quantity purchases by corporations, associations, and others.
For details, contact the publisher at the address above.

ISBN-13:   000-0-000000-00-0 (Paperback Version)
                      000-0-000000-00-0 (Digital Version)

REV. DATE: 24/03/2022

ACKNOWLEDGMENTS

This being the first of many flights of imagination, A discussion between a father and son about THE FATHER. I want to thank those without whom none of this would be possible.

First, I must give all Praise, Honor, and Glory to Christ who protects, guides, strengthens, and inspires me daily. You have made me the man I am and have blessed me with all that I have. I'm so unapologetically grateful for all that You are in my life. I am forever indebted and humbled by your Majesty, Power, and Mercy. Amen.

To my Mother, SGA: You have always been my biggest fan and my greatest supporter. You allowed me to reach for stars I could only imagine, and assured me they were there for me to grab onto if I only work hard and believe. You taught me better than anyone else could have, how to be a good man. I consider you my ultimate blessing because without your guidance and encouragement I might never have found my way. Yours is the example of strength, resilience, determination, and integrity that I draw from in my walk. I thank and Love you, Momma.

To the Brothers of Kappa Alpha Psi Fraternity Inc. I love all you guys and appreciate the bond we share in Phi Nu Pi. Your support and belief in my talents means the world to me and I can't thank you brothers enough for your help in bringing these dreams of mine to fruition. Nupe Nupe Yo!!!

This story is for the Fathers who have been Blessed with Sons of their own. My hope is that you would read this to your young Prince. To introduce them to not only a thirst for reading, but an Awesomely Wonderful God. Share with them His unconditional Love and full Knowledge of their entire Spirit. He desires only the most joyous lives possible for each and every one of us. All He asks from us is that we allow Him into our Hearts.

START A LEGACY OF FAITH!!!

When I was born, my Father said to me, "You are a Man, my Son. As such, you are my legacy in this world. All that I am can be seen in you, and all that you are is a reflection of me. For you are my Son."

When I was a child, my Father said to me, "You are a Man, my Son. You are of me and as such, you may look like me. You may speak like me… and at times you may even think the way I think. For you are my Son."

4

My father would say to me that as his son, I possessed certain abilities. He said that, I was special and He showed me how to do things in a way no one else could. He would say, "These gifts I give to only you. For you are my Son."

When I was a Young Boy, my Father said to me, "You are a Man, my Son. You are a part of my Family and as such, you will have Brothers and Sisters. You should Love them as I Love you all, unconditionally. For you are my Son."

My Father told me that, I was His favorite and that as such, He would show me Favor. He would say to me, "I will protect you and comfort you. For you are my Son."

My Father would say to me, "You are a Man, my Son. You are a good boy and as such, you should obey me. You are not perfect and may make mistakes, but ask me to, I will forgive you. For you are my Son."

At times my Father would test me. He said to Trust Him and that the things I experienced in life would build me, make me stronger and fortify my resolve. He would say, "Believe in me, I will sustain you. For you are my Son."

As I continued to grow, my Father listened to me. I would tell him my wants and needs. He would say to me, "I will provide you with all that you could ever need to be all that you could ever want. For you are my Son."

As a teenager, my Father would say to me, "You are a Man, my Son. As such, some day you will be filled with wisdom, but even as you become wiser, I will guide you. I will never leave you. For you are my Son."

As a young adult, my Father and I were separated. I fought for my independence, my individuality, my own way. My Father would say to me, "I care for you, my son… and as such, I must allow you to find the path I have set for you. I assure you it is there. For you are my Son."

My Father would say to me that, I am a Man. He said that as such, I should work hard. He told me, to never stop learning and striving to do my best... and that, although things might not come easy, I should know, He too is working for me. For He is my Father and I am His Son.

When we were reunited my Father said to me that, he had missed me. He said that, He had not forgotten me or given up on me, knowing that someday I would return to Him. This He knew because He is my Father and I am His Son.

My Father promised me that I would find a wife. He said that, she would be my partner in Life and that she would be made just for me. My Father said that, I was to love her unconditionally, protect her, and provide for her. He said that, I was to treat her as a gift to me, His Son.

Eventually, I had a son of my own. My Father told me that, I would raise him from a Prince to a King. He said that, I should teach him the things that He had taught me and that he too would have purpose. This He knew because He is my Father. I am His Son.

When my Dad passed away, my Father told me, to not Faint but to have Faith. He even said to me that, He would Restore my Heart and eventually even ease my Pain. This he promised me. For I am His Son.

My Father would tell me that, he was proud of me. He told me that, I had followed His path as He asked me to. Believed without Proof. Acted in spite of Fear and Trusted through Doubt. He told me that, he would Reward my deeds. Because I am His Son.

I would tell my son that he is a Man. I told him that he was my Legacy and all that was the best of me. I assured him that as such, he had a purpose and a path. I told him to follow my Father. This I told my Son, as my Father had told me.

And eventually it came to pass that, my Father called to me. He said that, my journey was now over. He said that, my mission had been fulfilled and that I could join Him as my Dad had. He had prepared a place for me, His son.

Thank you Father, for all that you have done, are doing, and will do in the Lives of your children. You are truly Worthy of all of the Worship, all of the Praise, and all of the Glory. Amen.

THE END

www.ingramcontent.com/pod-product-compliance
Lightning Source LLC
Chambersburg PA
CBHW041555120626
46551CB00002B/222